Strictly Murder

A play

Brian Clemens

Samuel French — London
www.samuelfrench-london.co.uk

STRICTLY MURDER

First presented at the Mill at Sonning Theatre on 21st
February 2006 with the following cast:

Josef	Jeffrey Perry
Peter Meredith	Nick Waring
Suzy Hinchcliffe	Maxine Gregory
Ross	Giles Watling
Miriam Miller	Clare Hatfield

Directed by Sally Hughes
Set designed by Jacqueline Hutson
Costumes designed by Jane Kidd
Lighting designed by Matthew Biss

CHARACTERS

Josef, middle-aged
Peter Meredith, 30-49
Suzy Hinchcliffe, young
Ross
Miriam Miller

Male Voice off stage (may be played by Ross)
Pre-recorded voices of British and German **Radio Announcers**

Note: when the German Radio Announcer speaks, licence should be taken so as to emphasise words vital for interpretation: i.e. "Hitler", "Reich", "Reichte des Vaterlands", "Der Führer". Recording of an Adolf Hitler speech can be obtained from BBC Radio for a small fee or from the Old Time Radio website: www.OTRCAT.com

SYNOPSIS OF SCENES

The action of the play takes place in a rustic cottage in a valley in Provence, France.

Time — 1939

ACT I

Scene 1 Early morning in April
Scene 2 Later that day
Scene 3 Some time later

ACT II

Scene 1 Morning. Five months later
Scene 2 Early evening. Later that day
Scene 3 That night

This play is dedicated to
my darling wife Janet
and our talented sons, George and Sam

Other plays by Brian Clemens
published by Samuel French Ltd:

Anybody for Murder? (*with Dennis Spooner*)
The Devil at Midnight
Edge of Darkness
Inside Job
Shock!
A Sting in the Tale (*with Dennis Spooner*)
Will You Still Love Me in the Morning? (*with Dennis Spooner*)

ACT I

Scene 1

A rural, stone built cottage situated in a valley in Provence. Dawn. April 1939

The set consists, in the main, of a kitchen/living area, where almost all social activity takes place

A stable door, in two halves, leads directly in from outside. Elsewhere an internal door or archway leads to all other areas of the cottage, including the rear

There is a largish window US, with practical sink, stove and cupboards beneath. The view through the window gives an impression of open country with trees beyond. Above or adjacent to the window is a bulkhead shelf where wine is stored. Near the sink is a waste bin. There is a small, rough hewn table DS, with a couple of wooden chairs. On the table is a bowl of fruit. Elsewhere in the area is a beaten-up old sofa with a few magazines and papers on it. Near the stable door is a free-standing hatstand that can barely be seen because, over time, it has accumulated a mound of coats, hats, scarves, etc. At its feet are Wellington boots, some with walking sticks or umbrellas stuck in them

There are a few pictures on the walls, all by the same artist and predominately of red poppies. Elsewhere some canvases are stacked against a wall. On the floor is a rough, woven rug that has seen better days. Somewhere in the area is an electric wireless of the period. There is electric light, but also an oil lamp for emergency lighting

As the CURTAIN rises it is still fairly dark, and the silence is profound. Somewhere, far off, a cock crows

A long moment. The top half of the stable door opens and Josef is revealed. His age is difficult to determine, he might be as young as 40, or as old as 60. There is a stoop of pain about him, he is shabbily dressed in "farmer's clothes" and, as we shall see, he is not mentally "normal", he can be almost childlike in his behaviour. Across one shoulder is slung a worn canvas bag.

He carries a shotgun or rifle. His movements are furtive and wary as he leans in, gently unbolts the lower half of the door, and enters

He moves deeper into the area, collides with a chair, freezes, looks around, then moves to open and delve into a cupboard. It is too dim to see, so he moves to switch on the lights, then homes in on a chunk of bread near the sink, bites into it, then notices the apples in the fruit bowl, grabs two, admires them, polishes them, slips them into his bag

With a squawk of sound, the wireless, being in tandem with the Lights, warms up and comes on. Josef swings his gun round towards the wireless in alarm. The radio signal is intermittent; French music of the period plays, but occasionally the station is lost and static intervenes. Josef stares at the wireless, then relaxes and carries on his search for food. He finds some grapes and pops some into his mouth, finds a can and pops it into his bag

Peter (*off*) Suzy?

Josef reacts, quickly moves to exit through the stable door, pulling it closed behind him

Peter Meredith enters through the internal door. He could be anything between 30 and 49, an attractive man with a face that is either cruel or has suffered. He is in stockinged feet, trousers, vest, and is just putting on a shirt

Suzy?

He seems surprised to find the place empty. He moves to the wireless, to adjust it to a clearer signal, until some classical music plays. This done, he now delves into cupboards to find cheese which, with the bread, he begins to assemble into an austere breakfast. He puts the kettle on to make coffee

The Lights suddenly flicker, dim, then go out altogether. The wireless stops too

Bloody thing! (*He moves to the hatstand and begins to step into some Wellington boots*) I'm not going to be kind to you this time. Going to kick you where it hurts most, you bloody awful, fickle, generator!

Even as he speaks, the Lights flicker and come on again, and a moment later the wireless comes back on, playing music

Lucky for you! (*He takes his food to the table, and sits to take alternate bites from the cheese and bread*)

The wireless loses station again; Peter rises to correct it

Male BBC Announcer Britain and France are now wholeheartedly pledged
   to defend Poland against attack should it come. In the House of Commons
   all parties endorsed Prime Minister Chamberlain when he asserted that…

The radio loses station again

*Peter re-tunes the wireless. During the following, Peter remains by the
wireless, listening intently. It is clear he understands German*

Male German Announcer Erneut versprach Reichskanzler Hitler die
   Unabhaengigkeit der Slowakei und verzichtete auf jegliche
   Gebietsansprueche. Erneut machte er geltend, daß sein einziges Ziel der
   Frieden in Europa sei, stellte aber gleichzeitig klar, dass sein Hauuptanliegen
   das "Reich" und die "Reichte des Vaterlands" waren und bleiben werden.
   Das Wetter hierzulande wird heute… [*Translation: Chancellor Hitler
   again promised independence for Slovakia, and discounted that he had
   any claims to the territory. He asserted again that his only aims were for
   peace in Europe, but at the same time made it clear that the Reichland and
   the rights of the Fatherland were, and would remain, his prime concen. On
   the Home Front—the weather today is expected to be…*]

Peter switches it off and returns to his breakfast

*The stable door rattles and Suzy Hinchcliffe enters. She is quite a lot
younger than Peter, with a fresh-faced, waif-like quality that makes her
vulnerable. Her clothes are drab, suitable for work, covered by a top coat*

Peter I thought we were supposed to be economizing. You know how much
   it costs to fuel that generator?
Suzy What brought this on?
Peter You left the lights on when you went to work.
Suzy I did not.
Peter They were on when I got up.
Suzy Well … perhaps I did. I overslept, had to run most of the way.
Peter Christ! What a miserable, unfeeling bastard I am.
Suzy I do wish you wouldn't swear.
Peter Can't help it, it's enough to make a saint spit blood. You going off in
   the early hours to clean up other peoples' messes.
Suzy That's the way hotels are run.
Peter Hotel? It's a pension with pretensions.
Suzy Darling, we need the money.

Peter I know, and that's what tears me up, you having to work, while I…? I just wish I could provide better for you.

Suzy I'm not complaining.

Peter No, you never do. You're Number One on my list. Mind you, it is a very short list.

Suzy I hope so.

Peter C'mon, sit down, I'll make you some breakfast.

Suzy No, thanks. Tell the truth I've been feeling a bit queasy. Anyway, I had a croissant up at the hotel.

Peter Mean buggers are feeding you now, are they?

Suzy No, that was Antoine. The breakfast chef.

Peter Antoine? You haven't mentioned him before.

Suzy He's new. Only been there the last month. (*During the following, she removes her coat and dumps it on to the hatstand*)

Peter And taken a shine to you, has he? You'll have coffee at least? (*He lifts the kettle and starts to make coffee*)

Suzy I think he'd be more likely to take a shine to you.

Peter Oh, he's like that, eh? I better be careful, then.

Suzy He saw you the other morning working in the field—stripped to the waist. He mentioned it.

Peter *Very* careful. Entranced by my manly body, was he?

Suzy Saw the scars on your back, and said a very curious thing.

Peter Oh?

Suzy Said they looked more like they'd been made by barbed wire, than in a car accident.

Peter almost slops the coffee he is pouring

Peter And what would he know! Stupid, snooping…! He should mind his own damned business!

Suzy (*a bit taken aback by his reaction*) He was only offering an opinion.

Peter He should keep his blasted opinions to himself and stop poking his nose where it doesn't belong!

Suzy Peter!

Peter (*calming down*) Sorry, but I've told you before how that accident affected me. I don't like to be reminded. You sure you wouldn't like a bit of breakfast?

Suzy I have to go out again later, I want to get changed.

Peter Better be making a move myself.

Suzy exits through the internal door

Peter starts to get ready to go out: dons a jacket, and boots. He starts to stack some paintings into a carrying bag. He takes down a top coat, then starts to search through the hatstand

(*Eventually*) Suzy?
Suzy (*off*) Yes?
Peter Darling, have you seen my beret?
Suzy (*off*) On the hatstand.
Peter There's everything on the stand except the kitchen sink, *and* my beret!
Suzy (*off*) Probably stuffed into a wellie.

Peter searches through the boots and finds his beret crushed into one, smoothes it, dons it at a jaunty angle

Peter Got it.
Suzy (*off*) Don't know why you bother.
Peter It impresses the customers. A masterpiece from the brush of a local artist.
Suzy (*off*) Local!?
Peter If they are Brits, or better still, Americans, I put on a bit of the "haw-haw-haw" *and* the beret. Give them the whole Chevalier: "Madam admires zee way I have painted zee poppies?" It can add a few francs to the sale.

Suzy enters through the internal door. She has changed her dress to something a bit brighter

Suzy And a few extra francs are always welcome.
Peter I'm feeling lucky today, the sun is threatening to shine. Customers—if there are any—will be in a spending mood. Yes indeed, I really have that lucky feeling!
Suzy You wouldn't mind walking to the market, then?
Peter Eh?
Suzy I have to go to Digne, and I'd like to take the car.
Peter The car? You mean "Le Heap", don't you? But take it by all means, the walk will do me good.
Suzy (*pecking him on the cheek*) Thanks, darling. (*She takes a scarf from the hatstand*)
Peter What's in Digne, anyway?
Suzy (*hesitating*) We desperately need some new bedsheets and I can get them straight from the factory there. At a discount.
Peter Good thinking. (*He hefts his bag*) I'll be off, then.
Suzy You've just put it right out of your mind, haven't you? What we were talking about last night. Have you thought any more about us?

Peter puts his bag down again

Peter Suzy, you know how much I love you…
Suzy But not enough to marry me.
Peter We've been through all that. I will marry you, someday, but not now with the world in such a mess, and a war coming…
Suzy You can't know that for sure.
Peter You've heard the reports, there are all the signs…
Suzy Antoine says Hitler only wants to reclaim land he regards as rightfully German.
Peter Antoine? What would he know!?
Suzy He says that if Hitler had aggressive intentions there would already be German agents here in France, doing sabotage. There hasn't been any evidence of that, has there?

Peter regards her for a moment

Peter If there were agents here, don't you think they'd be secret, undercover.
Suzy Oh, come on, Peter.
Peter Hitler has his intentions, you don't know the man.
Suzy And you do, I suppose?
Peter No, of course not, but reading between the lines…
Suzy You're just using it as an excuse not to commit.
Peter Any fool can see that his ambitions are much wider.
Suzy But I'm not any fool, Peter, I'm the woman who shares your bed.
Peter Suzy… *Suzy*. A band of gold won't make me love you any more than I already do.
Suzy No, but it would stop me feeling like a … a scarlet woman! You know, back home in England my friends and family would shun me.
Peter But you're not back home. We're here in France, they're more tolerant here, there's no stigma here. Darling…

He moves to embrace and kiss her, until she moves away

Suzy Nothing will make you change your mind, then?
Peter I'm sorry.
Suzy That's what you always say.
Peter But I *am* sorry, and I want to try to make you understand… (*He pauses*) Look, go and get your bedsheets, and while you're at it… (*He produces some franc notes, presses them into her hand*) Buy something for yourself, eh? A hat or—whatever, some luxury for *you*. Something to perk you up.

Suzy looks at the money in her hand

Suzy So now I'm a *paid* scarlet woman.
Peter Oh, Suzy… (*Lost for words, he picks up his bag again*) I have to go. See you tonight, eh?

Peter exits through the stable door

Suzy gazes after him

Suzy Yes. I'll see you tonight.

Suzy moves to shut the stable door, and exits through the internal door

A long pause, then Josef's face appears at the window, and disappears again. A moment later the stable door opens and Josef enters

As before, he is furtive, looking around, then moving in to pour himself some coffee, savours it, then he puts his gun down near the hatstand, sits at the table and begins to pick at the remains of Peter's breakfast

As Josef reaches for an apple and bites into it, Suzy enters through the internal door. She sees Josef and very carefully moves in to pick up the gun and creep in on Josef from behind until she is inches away, the gun pointing at his head

Got you!

Josef jumps a mile in alarm—getting up, almost falling, spinning round in the same movement and shoving his hands behind his back

Show me your hands. *Your hands!*

Reluctantly Josef shows his hands, one holding the apple. Suzy lowers the gun

Oh, Josef, we've told you before about this stupid pilfering.

Josef makes to put the half eaten apple back in the bowl, but she swings the gun back at the aim

No!

Josef stands there, helplessly

You stole an apple. Do you remember who brought those apples? Do you?

You brought them, Josef, do you remember that? You brought them to us as a gift. So you were stealing from yourself. You silly, silly man.

Josef hangs his head

Why do you do it, Josef?

Josef I... I don't know why... I think it's to...

Suzy Yes?

Josef It's to show me that I can! To stay ... alert. In ... trim. (*He seems pleased to have remembered this*)

Suzy Well, it has to stop, understand? And you have got to start knocking on that door or one day you'll give me a heart attack. (*She tosses the gun back to him*)

Josef I'm sorry.

Suzy I'm sure you are.

Josef I didn't mean to frighten you...

Suzy I know you didn't, but you still keep on doing it. You know you're always welcome here, Josef, I've made that clear many times. So has Peter.

Josef Peter. He's my friend.

Suzy And you are ours. But you must try to behave like one.

Josef Peter's done a lot for me. So have you.

Suzy We would like to do more. Why don't you leave that old hovel of yours and move into our barn? It's not the Ritz, but the roof doesn't leak, and it would be a great deal more comfortable than where you are now. And warmer.

Josef I... I feel ... safer where I am. Divide and conquer. (*He giggles*) I think Peter said that. I think.

Suzy I've no idea what you are talking about, and I doubt you do either. Would you like some breakfast?

Josef I already have. I found a toad.

Suzy Don't tell me you ate a toad?!

Josef They eat toads here.

Suzy No, Josef, they eat frogs. Never toads. You shouldn't kill toads.

Josef I didn't kill it. I've got it in my pocket, would you like to see it?

Suzy I think not. Just take it back to where you found it, Josef, we never begrudge sharing what little we have, you know that. All you have to do is ask. *Knock on the door and ask.* Will you do that in future? And no more sneaking about like a thief in the night.

Josef But it's daylight...

Suzy Promise me.

Josef I'll... I'll try.

Suzy I'm just about to drive over to Digne, would you like to come along? Peter gave me enough to treat us both to lunch.

Josef Digne?

Suzy I'd like the company, and to tell the truth, I'm always waiting for that old car of ours to break down and leave me stranded. Having someone along—even if it's only you—would make me feel more comfortable. I mean, if the worst comes to the worst, you can at least *push*, can't you?

Josef Digne?

Suzy And this is a special day for me, Josef, I can't tell you why yet, but it is. What do you say? You can even bring your toad.

Josef I don't like to be "off watch" too long.

Suzy Off watch? All you do it sit on that hill waiting for a hare or a fox or something, I've never known you shoot anything, and I don't think you ever could. Well?

Josef I'll ... think about it.

Suzy Well, don't think too long, I'll be off in a couple of minutes. (*She moves towards the internal door, pauses*) Divide and conquer? What did that mean?

Josef I dunno. I forget things. Take care of each other! Yes. Like ... like family.

Suzy Have you got family, Josef?

Josef Not any more. I think. I think I was married once. Yes!

Suzy Married? Do you have children?

Josef Children?

It gnaws at him

Children!

Suzy Oh, Josef...! I'll be back in a moment.

Suzy exits through the internal door

Josef Children? *Children!* (*He covers his face with his hands for a moment, then looks around in some desperation—then suddenly moves to hide behind the sofa*)

Suzy enters through the internal door, carrying a purse, etc., ready to go out

Suzy Josef? (*She looks around, opens the stable door*) Josef!

Puzzled, Suzy sighs, switches off the lights, and exits through the stable door

A moment, then we hear a car door slam—then the tinny engine sound of an

*old car starting up and moving away. Josef emerges from behind the sofa. He
has the run of the place and is not sure what to do first. He switches on the
lights. Moves to pour and swig some coffee. Bite into bread and apple. Then
strolls over to the wireless, switches it on and moves to sit down and continue
eating in comfort. The wireless warms up*

Male German Announcer Gestern Abend hat der Führer die
Menschenmenge von mehr als fünfzig tausend trewen Deutsch angeredet,
vowärts seinem Traum einen besseren Reich zu stellen ... [*Translation:
Last night the Fuhrer addressed a crowd of more than fifty thousand loyal
Germans, to put forward his dream of a better Reichsland...*]

*This is followed by an extract from one of Hitler's speeches/tirades at its most
dramatic. The effect on Josef is astonishing, he stands up from the table, and
seems to become another, different man, standing proudly, stiffly to attention,
clicking his heels together, raising his arm in the Nazi salute and*

Josef Heil Hitler!

Black-out

SCENE 2

The Lights come up on the cottage. About an hour later

*It is silent and empty, then BANG! The stable door crashes open and Peter
enters in a rush, closes the door, leans against it. He is panting, sweating,
dishevelled, but still clutches his bag*

*He gets his breath, takes off his topcoat and beret, tosses them on to the
hatstand, hurries over to the window to look out, then turns, unsure for a
moment what to do. He is galvanized into action as he rushes around, taking
the poppy paintings down and stuffing them into his bag or out of sight. He
then stows the bag away behind the hatstand*

*He returns to the window to gaze out again, then hurries to pick up a long
carving knife, hefts it, regards it for a moment, and his gaze shifts from knife
to the wine bottles in their bulkhead rack. He puts down the knife and moves
to slide bottles in and out until he finds the bottle of Château Latour he was
looking for*

He uncorks it, but, as is the way of things in situations of urgency, it does not immediately pull out. Finally it does. He reaches up to the topmost shelf, that bears flit sprays, bottles and packets, he takes down a fairly large one— clearly poisonous, as it bears a warning cross or a death's head logo

He kneels at a cupboard to rummage furiously until he finds a funnel. He takes the funnel and the packet to the wine—puts the funnel into the bottle— hesitates—takes the funnel out again, pours a generous glass of the wine, sets it aside, puts the funnel in the bottle again and tips in a large measure of powder from the packet. He lightly re-corks the bottle, places it near to the full glass, then places the funnel and the packet at the back of the sink

Throughout these actions he from time to time peeks out of the window. The actions completed, he again looks out of the window, and this time reacts to whoever is coming, by stepping back and away from the window, without ever taking his eyes off it

Then, still thinking on his feet, he adjusts his appearance, flattens his tousled hair down with both hands, makes an effort to control his breathing and settles himself down on a chair. He thinks better of it and moves to sit on the sofa, pick up a magazine and affect to be reading it—to look relaxed

A long moment, and then there is a knock at the door

Ross (*off*) Hallo, hallo, anyone home?
Peter *Entré—la porte est ouvert.* [*Translation: Come on in, the door's open*]

The stable door opens and Ross stands framed in it. He is perhaps 40, a tall, prepossessing man with a feeling of great strength about him. The sort of man who can dominate a room by just entering it. His voice is cultured, his manners impeccable to the point of smarminess. He is unsuitably dressed for hiking in the region: a well-cut dark suit, waistcoat, white shirt, club tie perfectly tied, plus a dark hat, a trilby or a bowler. He looks the personification of a ranking police officer in mufti, probably from Scotland Yard. He has walked some way in these clothes, and appears somewhat distressed

Ross Pardon me. *Parlez-vous anglais?*

Peter gets to his feet

Peter *Oui, M'siur, je parlais anglais.* Matter of fact I am English.
Ross Thank goodness for that, old boy. My French! It's a long time since I conjugated a verb, and frankly, I was more of a rugger man.

Peter How can I help you?

Ross Well. First I took a stroll in the woods, in the jolly old bois, then I got lost, and then I got *very* thirsty … saw your little cottage and … I could kill for a glass of water.

Peter Killing won't be necessary I hope. (*He goes to get water and pours a glass*)

Ross Damned silly of me to start walking at all, in these clothes. Didn't expect to get so hot at this time of the year.

Peter That's Provence for you, the climate can be full of surprises.

Ross Getting lost too, I usually pride myself on my sense of direction. I'll need you to point me back to the town. After I've sat for a spell, if you don't mind?

Peter Not at all. (*He proffers a glass of water, hesitates*) If you would prefer a glass of wine?

Ross Just the old H₂O, for the dried-out old bod. I'm absolutely parched. (*He takes the glass, drains it, proffers it for more*) Adam's ale. Do you mind?

Peter recharges the glass with water, Ross is about to drink, but…

Oh, but my manners, old boy. Name's Ross.

Peter Peter Meredith.

Ross Used to know a Meredith at Stowe. Damned fine fly half. You wouldn't be…?

Peter No relation I'm afraid. We were more Grammar School.

Ross Oh, well, never mind, takes all sorts. (*Sipping his water, he looks around*) Charming little place you have here, Mr Meredith, and of course, when it's properly done up…

Peter It *is* done up.

Ross Ah, I see. Commune with the rustics, eh? Back to dear old Mother Nature.

Peter (*without rancour*) I don't really see that it is any of your business.

Ross Quite so, old boy. Absolutely right.

Peter But actually this is all I can afford just now.

Ross I understand, and if you are happy here, eh? That's the main thing.

Peter I've always felt … secure here.

Ross Admirable criterion, security in these uncertain times. Yes, I approve of that "Englishman's home is his castle" and all that. Funny how people differ though, how they settle for one thing and not the other. I once knew a man who was offered fifty thousand sterling—or was it Reichmarks? Whatever, it was a large sum of money, small fortune in fact, and all this man had to do was co-operate with the authorities and point them towards a fugitive. Blighter turned it down flat. What do you think of that?

Peter I imagine he had his reasons.

Ross Yes, though damned stupid if you ask me. What do you do, Mr Meredith? Out here in isolation and, if you will forgive me saying so, obviously not of independent means. How do you survive?

Peter I ... help out during the fruit and grape season, do a bit of driving for a local farmer.

Ross That's odd. I bumped into a peasant type on my way here, and he seemed to think you were some kind of artist. A painter.

Peter Oh, I dabble. A Sunday painter, more for my own amusement.

Ross rises and moves to look out of the window   action

Ross Apart from that little hotel on the hill there appears to be nothing and no-one for miles. You must like your own company? Or do you have a ... companion?

Peter There is a woman.

Ross Yes, my peasant type told me that too. A woman, and conveniently she appears to be out at the moment. Does she know that your name isn't really Meredith?

Peter She knows nothing, do you hear, nothing! She is not involved in any way.

Ross Hmm, well, we'll see. Hate to doubt your word, understand, but you have to admit, you have been a bit of a naughty old fibber in the past. *(His marshmallow bluffness is falling away, to reveal the sheer, professional steel beneath)* I am, of course, armed. *(He produces a revolver from his pocket)*

Peter You won't need that.

Ross Shall I not? You are a dangerous and callous man. But you're right. *(He drops the gun back into his pocket)* Took you once, and I can take you again. Eh, Giles? *(He moves closer to Peter to "inspect" him)* Giles Hudson. You have changed a great deal since you left my tender care. But that was to be expected. Losing the beard, changing the colour of your hair, yes, I anticipated that. But your face...? There has been some subtle facial surgery. Quite transforming, I don't think I would have recognized you. Who arranged it, that doctor friend of yours? It's quite brilliant, the signs of a broken nose is a particularly splendid touch.

Peter If you recall, I broke my nose while in *your* "tender care".

Ross You only have yourself to blame, you were a *very* recalcitrant prisoner ... but you've come far, you must have had some expert assistance along the way. You wouldn't care to tell me? No? Never mind, we'll find out who helped you to escape, etcetera, etcetera, and of course, they will be caught and punished too. Yes, we'll get it right this time.

Peter We? Tweedledum and Tweedledee. Which one are you?

Ross Does it matter?

Peter Not really.

Ross Yes, it's wise to be pragmatic about the whole afrair. It's been a long time, Giles—what—four years?

Peter Four years, two months, six days.

Ross Some were convinced that you had run to South Africa—or even returned to Germany. Not me. Others thought you had gone to ground in Britain—sheltered by friends. But you don't have any friends, do you, Giles? They disowned you after they learned of your brutal double murder—your wife *and* child. I always thought *Europe*. With your knowledge of the Continent…

Peter How did you find me?

Ross You won't believe me, I scarcely can myself… Serendipity. Good fortune. A happy accident. You see, I wasn't actually looking for you at the time. Naturally one keeps one's eyes open, but I had just finished exhaustive inquiries in Paris, and thought I deserved a little break, so decided to visit some friends in Perpignan. So there I am, chuff-chuffing through the French countryside, it's nearly time for luncheon, and the food on the train most unappealing. Then I looked out of the window and saw your little town coming up; saw the square, and what appeared to be a charming little restaurant.

Peter The Montmartre.

Ross You know it? But of course you do! Anyway, on a sudden whim I decided to break my journey and take luncheon at the Montmartre.

Peter And you saw the paintings.

Ross The owner told me that you exchanged them for food and supplies. Oh, Giles, you can disguise your looks, but not your style and obsession with poppies. The walls of your cell were covered in them. I realized right away, and then the restaurant owner told me that you had a pitch in the market, not one hundred metres from where I was sitting. I saw you immediately, and that, I think, is when *you* saw me? Seren-dipity-doo-dah! I can hardly believe such out-of-the-blue luck. I tell you, old boy, I can't wait to hear their reaction when I tell them to call off the search—to see their faces when I take you in.

Peter You haven't told them yet, then?

Ross There hasn't been time, and anyway, as you well know, I am a most thorough man, I had to be quite sure it was you. I must confess though, I was mildly disappointed.

Peter Disappointed?

Ross You gave in so very easily. When I appeared at that door why didn't you just pretend that "Peter Meredith" was out, and you were just a local friend? I know your French is good enough to have fooled me.

Peter I can disguise my face, but not my voice. Anyway, the minute I looked into your eyes I knew that *you* knew, and it was hopeless.

Ross Yes, I'm a dogged old bugger, am I not?! "Dogged" is a good word; a dog on the scent, a dog worrying away at a bone it is never going to let go of. And you were that bone, Giles.

Peter What happens now?

Ross (*patting his pocket*) I still have the gun, but as you said, I won't need it, will I? You will precede me to the station—very carefully.

Peter You wouldn't kill me.

Ross Not in my remit, old boy—or our best interests. No, a leg wound would be sufficient, and I am a crack shot. Oh, but it won't come to that. Will it?

Peter seems to slump his shoulders in despair—all the fight gone out of him

Peter You've won, as I suppose I always knew you would some day. (*He wanders away to pick up the glass of wine to drink*)

Ross snatches it from him   glass of wine

You wouldn't begrudge me?

Ross takes a tiny sip from the glass, savours it, then grabs and examines the bottle

Ross A Château Latour! When did you open this?

Peter Last night, we were celebrating a sale.

Ross By Godfrey, it's almost as though you were expecting me. Pour me a glass.

Peter But shouldn't we be…?

Ross (*overriding*) Pour me a glass!

Peter pours a glass for Ross, who holds it to the light; sniffs the bouquet   Pause

I haven't had a decent Latour in—well, too long. It is my favourite wine, you know.

Peter Yes, I knew that.

Ross smiles, taps his glass against Peter's

Ross To our long overdue reunion. "Goodbye Piccadilly, farewell Leicester Square"! For you anyway.

They drink

Mmm. I get the blackcurrants, the rich red earth and a *whisper* of plum. (*He sips away*) But there's something else beneath them all … something darker, more potent … not sure … but I'll get it eventually. (*He finishes the glass, proffers it for more*) *Pour*

Peter recharges the glass

You were always my favourite prisoner, Giles—resilient, you knew so much and gave so little. But four years is a long time, techniques have changed, improved. It'll be a pleasure once I have you behind bars again, to sit and chat and resume our relationship (*He continues drinking*) Ah, I almost had it then … but no… If I hadn't seen the label I might have said it was something chemical … but in a Latour!? Impossible. Whatever it is, it's growing on me. (*He finishes the glass, proffers for yet another*)

Peter pours more wine

You won't get me drunk, you know. If that is your intention.
Peter You're the one asking for more.
Ross Yes. Well, just the same. Few weeks ago I took a friend to my club for luncheon. Started with Champagne aperitifs, Chablis with the oysters, and a sturdy Burgundy with the meat. Followed by several Armagnacs. An hour later I was on the range, taking the pips out of the bullseye! No, you won't ever get me drunk.
Peter It was not my aim to get you drunk. In fact, I wasn't even sure that you'd fall for the wine.
Ross Fall for?
Peter Or even if I intended it for you or me.
Ross What are you talking about?
Peter Was I going to kill you—or me? I was never really sure on that point—in fact, until now, I think suicide had the edge.
Ross Suicide?
Peter I am never going back to your prison, Ross. That's one thing I *am* sure of.

Ross moves towards him, then staggers slightly, clutches the sofa to get his balance

Ross What are you saying?
Peter You were right about that dark, potent under-taste, it *is* chemical.
Ross What? What!? (*He is starting to be terribly affected by the poison*)
Peter Or chemi*cals*. Strychnine is one, I know that, but there are others.
Ross Chemicals?
Peter In the rat poison, that's what you've been drinking, Ross, a fine Château Latour, laced with rat poison.

Ross Rat poison…? But it will kill me.
Peter That's the general idea. Old boy.

Ross makes a huge effort to pull the gun from his pocket, but Peter closes with him, they struggle, during which, Ross's hat falls from the arm of the sofa to the floor. The struggle ends when Peter pushes free, now in possession of the gun. Ross tries to move to him, clutching at the sofa   FIGHT

Ross This isn't right, I'm the law. The law. And you…? You're a fugitive   settee
from… Justice…
Peter No, I'm the Grim Reaper, bringing you *and* me a happy release.

FIGHT.

Ross bellows, tries to go for Peter, doesn't make it, and falls to the floor behind the sofa, leaving just his legs projecting

Ross Pity, have pity.   – on floor.
Peter You talk to me of pity? You! You're taking too long to die, Ross, and
I have much to do. (*He aims the gun, then hesitates*) No, even here it might
be heard. (*He pockets the gun again—then kneels astride of Ross behind
the sofa, so that only his upper body is seen as he strangles Ross*)

We hear Ross's strangled cries becoming gurgles—and see his feet thrashing and drumming on the floor. Eventually the cries cease and Ross's limbs become still. Peter remains astride him for a long, long moment, until he is sure he is dead. Then he gets to his feet and, panting, regards the body

Now, fuelled by nervous energy, he goes to work with a meticulous precision: He empties the wine bottle into the sink, rinses it out, along with the two glasses. The bottle goes into the waste bin, the glasses back on a shelf. He wipes the gun clean with a tea cloth, hesitates, then wraps the gun in the cloth, pulls a wine bottle out of the bulkhead shelf, shoves the wrapped gun in the back, replaces the wine bottle

He returns to search the body, and comes up with a wallet, which he opens, and pulls out a wad of money, hesitates, then thrusts money into his pocket, replaces the wallet and goes to the window to look out left and right. Satisfied, he returns to the body, grabs the rug off the floor, and moves to wrap the body in it

Another look out of the window, then Peter exits through the internal door

A long moment—during which, hopefully, we notice that Ross's hat still lies where it fell

Josef enters through the stable door, not furtively this time, but proudly, carrying a bunch of wild flowers

He looks around, not certain where to put them, and finally decides and puts them into the fruit bowl—prominently atop of the fruit. He steps back to admire it, then sees Ross's hat on the floor. Delightedly, he moves to pick it up and put it on—mockingly bowing and doffing the hat—on—off—on…and then he sees Ross's body! He drops the hat, near or under the table, steps back, freezes in fear. Hesitates, steps closer to the body, and finally forces himself to lift one of Ross's limp arms, feels for a pulse—and drops the arm back again. He seems bewildered, studying the body, and then, in trepidation, he lifts the rug to look at the face. His reaction is profound—he scuttles back and away to the door, remains there a moment, making little sounds of alarm

Josef turns and exits through the stable door, leaving it open

A pause, then Peter enters through the internal door, doing up a pair of faded blue dungarees

He stops as he sees the open door, moves to it, pushes it wide and peers off in both directions. He closes the door and turns to survey the area, and sees the flowers. He moves to pick them up, regards them, wondering, looking around, finally drops them back on to the bowl, and moves to find a bottle of brandy, opens it and takes a long slug that has him coughing. It seems to calm him, and again he moves back to regard the flowers

Peter The door wasn't latched properly—wind must have blown it open. And these *flowers were* here this morning. Weren't they? Talking to yourself, first sign of panic, and that won't do. No, it won't do. Get a grip, get a grip!

He hurries away to grab the brandy again and takes another long swig, before returning the bottle to the draining board of the sink. He again surveys the scene, moves to look at the body, bends to pull it fully out from behind the sofa, regards it, then crouches beside it, to wrap, roll it into the rug

As he does this, Josef appears at the window, watching him

Unaware, Peter completes rolling Ross in the rug then as he starts to drag/ hoist the body towards the door…

Black-out

SCENE 3

The Lights come up on the cottage, some time later

The place is empty. Ross's body, and the rug, have gone. We hear the sound of a shovel being propped outside the stable door

It opens, Peter enters. His clothes, hands and face are muddy now. He carries a sack, and proceeds to take down the few poppy paintings around the room, and puts them in the sack, leaves the sack near the door, exits through the internal door

A moment, then Josef enters through the stable door, holding a shovel. He looks around then moves to the sofa, to gaze down at where the body once was

Peter enters through the internal door, carrying a medium sized paper sack. He is mildly surprised to see Josef

Peter Josef?
Josef What have you been up to?
Peter Up to?
Josef (*he lifts the shovel*) I found this outside the door.
Peter That's because I left it there. I haven't finished yet.
Josef Finished what?
Peter I've been digging out the cesspit.
Josef (*pointing at the sack*) What's that?
Peter This—it's quick-lime.
Josef Quick-lime? What's it for?
Peter It's in the interests of sanitation, Josef. It cleanses.
Josef Gets rid of bad things?
Peter Yes, you could say that.

Josef moves back to stare at where the body was

Josef, why are you here?
Josef I wanted to make sure.
Peter Sure of what?
Josef That you were still here. You won't go away, will you, you won't leave me?
Peter Only if someone made me, and that isn't likely any more.
Josef If someone tried to make you leave I'd stop them.
Peter I know, old fellow.

Josef stares where the body was

What's wrong?

Josef I don't know. I seem to remember ... something.

Peter You're having one of your memory lapses again. Well, let's try this one—you brought these flowers, didn't you?

Josef For Suzy. She's kind.

Peter And when did you bring them? Was it this morning?

Josef I ... don't remember. (*He stares at where the body was*) There's lots I don't remember.

Peter That can be a blessing.

Josef It *was* this morning! I saw Suzy. She gave me an apple ... or did I take it?

Peter Don't try too hard, old son. Now, do you want to hang on and make yourself some coffee? I have to finish up.

Josef She gave me an apple, and it was nice. I brought the flowers ... and then ... then... Why can't I remember?

Peter If it's important, it'll come. You know where the coffee is...

Josef Let me help you!

Peter No. Josef, this is something I must do alone. Anyway, it's messy and ... well, I'm almost done anyway. Do you understand? (*He makes to take the shovel*)

Josef evades him

Josef! (*He takes the shovel from him*)

Josef I could — stand guard!

Peter That's a good idea, you go up on to your hill and stand guard.

Josef Then nobody can take you away. Yes!

Josef happily exits through the stable door

Peter hefts the shovel, the sack containing lime and the bag of paintings and exits through the stable door

A long pause, then the stable door opens and Suzy enters. She looks and behaves wearily, moving to the hatstand to divest her top coat and scarf. She reacts to Peter's coat and beret there, picks the beret up and examines it, looks around

Suzy Peter!

Silence. She puts the beret aside, turns, then sees the flowers, picks them up, regards and sniffs them, smiling. Then she frowns, and moves to the spot where the rug once lay

Peter!

As she turns back, she sees or kicks against Ross's hat lying near or under the table. She picks it up, looks inside the brim and, puzzled, pops it on to the hatstand. She returns to sit at the table, puts her head in her hands for a moment

This won't do.

More briskly now, she moves to the sink and stove, takes down cups, coffee, etc., and moves between the sink and the table as she lays up for supper. Then the mood deserts her and, her back to us, she leans against the sink, her shoulders slumping as she silently weeps. Then she becomes aware of the open brandy bottle sitting on the draining board. She picks it up, anger replacing tears

The stable door opens. Peter enters, heading towards the internal door

Peter!

Peter spins round, utterly startled to find her there

Peter Suzy! Good God, I didn't hear the car.
Suzy You didn't hear it because it broke down half a mile from here!
Peter And you had to hike it? Darling, I am sorry...
Suzy What's been going on here?
Peter Going on? What do you mean...?
Suzy (*flourishing the bottle*) You've been drinking brandy at this time of day, *and where is the rug!*
Peter Rug?
Suzy Yes, you know—that faded thing that usually sits on the floor there?!
Peter Oh, you mean the *rug*? I chucked it.
Suzy Oh? A rich aunt died, did she? You've inherited a fortune?!
Peter Darling, you said yourself it was faded—and worn through too, way past its best.
Suzy Peter...
Peter (*overriding*) And, as a matter of fact, I have made some money. Not a fortune, but enough for a new rug and lots more beside. I made a big sale ... look. (*He pulls out Ross's wad of notes*)

Suzy stares at it, the wind taken out of her sails now, her anger dissipating a little

A real, live American—with a restaurant "back in California" that he calls the "Desert Poppy". Wants to decorate it with poppies. Bought all my stuff. (*He gestures at the empty walls*) I was drinking, to celebrate! Well, what do you think?

Suzy It couldn't have come at a better time.

Peter For us, any time is a better time. We'll get the car fixed, you'll be able to buy some new clothes… Come on, darling… (*He moves to embrace her*)

She remains a moment, then gently pulls free

Suzy I'd better get supper.

Peter No, we'll go out, celebrate some more—together. I won't have you cooking tonight, you'll be pampered, wined and dined. Eh? Eh? (*He grabs her again, lifts her face to him*) What do you say?

Suzy I suppose we could pop into town, go to the Montmartre.

Peter No, not the Montmartre.

Suzy Why not? It's an easy walk and not too expensive.

Peter I've been hearing complaints, the standard's gone down.

Suzy But you're always telling me how excellent they are——

Peter (*interjecting*) Tell you what, why don't we trek up to your hotel, have 'em wait on you for a change? And if this, whatever his name is… Antoine—if he's there I can send him mad with desire!

Suzy No. We ought to stay home.

Peter But, darling…

Suzy We can put that money to better use than dining out.

Peter Just one little fling?

Suzy No. We have to think to the future now.

Peter All right, if you say so. But we can at least use that whole shank of ham in one go, make it a feast … we can open that tin of truffles!

Suzy I was saving them for a special occasion.

Peter Well, today *is* special, isn't it?

Suzy Yes. In a way I suppose it is.

Peter Fine! OK, you direct me, I'll be your slave, commis chef, whatever…

Suzy smiles, unwinding at last

Suzy Very well, slave. Go and fetch the ham from the larder.

Peter (*bowing*) Your every wish, Madam, is my command.

Peter exits through the internal door

Suzy shakes her head, smiling after him, then turns back to the cupboards to begin taking out spices and ingredients. Then she finds the packet of rat poison—reacts in consternation

Peter enters through the internal door, carrying a wrapped ham

Suzy You could have killed someone, right here in this room!

Peter What?

Suzy (*flourishing the poison*) This, rat poison, left here where food is prepared!

Peter Oh damn, I thought I'd put it away... I'm sorry——

Suzy (*overriding*) Can you imagine if a cat or—or a child got hold of this?

Peter We don't have a cat, or a child for that matter.

Suzy Josef then, you know how he goes poking into everything, you know what I mean. What's it doing here, anyway?

Peter I didn't want you to find out...

Suzy Find out?

Peter Alarm you, then... I've been working on the cesspit and, well... I found some traces of rats.

Suzy Oh, Peter, *no*!

Peter It's OK, just traces, I'm sure they're long gone, but I thought it best to be sure, so I laid down some of that stuff, enough to knock over an elephant. If there are any rats, that'll take care of them in no time.

Suzy Down by the cesspit?

Peter Yes.

Suzy But nothing here in the house?

Peter Not a sign. I promise you.

Suzy (*shuddering*) Just the same, it was completely irresponsible. I'm not having this around any more. (*She bends to dispose of the poison in the waste bin—then reacts—and picks out the empty Latour bottle, studies it, straightens up, holding it high*) Peter, how could you?! *Our* Latour, that we scrimped and saved to buy and put aside.

Peter Darling, there is still one other bottle—there. (*He points to the bulkhead and wine, behind which the gun is concealed*)

Suzy That's not the point, we agreed not to open either of them until there was something *momentous*—and I don't call selling a few pictures—momentous.

Peter It was a big sale.

Suzy But not momentous.

Peter OK, I was wrong, but I was feeling euphoric... I've been in the doldrums quite a while...

Suzy (*interjecting*) We both have.

Peter What can I say? I'm sorry.

Suzy A whole bottle, you drank the whole bottle.

Peter Not quite, Josef dropped by and he helped me out. Also... Well, I spilt some. On the rug.

Suzy A whole bottle of Château Latour, *and* brandy.

Peter We were celebrating.

Suzy Celebrating? It sounds more like a drunken orgy!

Peter (*raising placating hands*) Darling... Suzy... Peace? (*He takes her hands*) I know what I did was selfish, thoughtless, but don't let it spoil our evening? We can still have our little feast.

Suzy I'm not hungry any more.

Peter Suzy, please...

Suzy No, no, it's not this—or you, I'm really not in the mood for food just now.

Peter Perhaps later?

Suzy Yes, later.

Peter But you will have a glass of wine with me?

Suzy I should think you've had enough.

Peter Oh, come on—one. Drink to my good fortune. *Our* good fortune? You won't refuse that?

Suzy Very well. A small glass.

Peter That's my girl. (*He moves to the bulkhead store*) Momentous or not, we do at least have a few francs to spare now. (*His hand hovers over the bottle of Latour*)

Suzy No!

Peter grins, takes down another bottle nearby

Peter Vin ordinaire, for a day extraordinaire! (*He sets to, opening the bottle, pouring two glasses*)

Suzy What did Josef want?

Peter Eh?

Suzy Josef, you said he dropped by, what did he want?

Peter What does he ever want? Nothing in particular, he just drops by.

Suzy Yes, he was here this morning.

Peter To bring you the flowers.

Suzy No. That must have been later. Didn't he bring them when he came to see you?

Peter No. (*He pauses in his labour, to look at the flowers*)

Suzy Must have been some other time, then.

Peter Yes, some other time.

Suzy That's three times in one day, then. You ought to discourage him from just popping in whenever he wants. Sometimes he scares me.

Peter Josef is quite harmless.

Suzy I know that. He wouldn't hurt a fly—or a toad.

Peter A toad?

Suzy I mean literally, he startles me with his jack-in-the-box antics, you never know just when or where he's going to appear. One day he could come in at a very inopportune moment.

Peter (*pausing*) Yes, you're right. I'll talk to him about it. (*Wine poured, he hands her a glass*) What'll it be? Prosit? Santé? Or us?

Suzy Us. All of us.

They clink glasses and drink

Was that when he brought the hat?

Peter Eh?

Suzy Josef—when he dropped by, was that when he brought the hat?

Peter What hat?

Suzy That hat. (*She points to Ross's hat on the hatstand*)

Peter freezes, staring at it

I don't think Josef exactly steals things, but it looks like the kind of object he might "acquire".

Peter No, I found it. On my way back from market, on the back road.

Suzy Found it? It's a funny thing for someone to lose.

Peter Oh, I dunno, chap's walking, high wind...

Suzy Wind or not, I can't imagine an expensively dressed man walking the back road. It doesn't lead anywhere, except to us.

Peter How do you arrive at "expensively dressed"?

Suzy moves to take down the hat

Suzy I don't know about the rest of him, but his head was. Didn't you read the label inside? "Gulliver's, New Bond Street".

Peter takes the hat from her, examines it

That probably cost more than our monthly food bill.

Peter (*laughing—making light of it*) I'll give it to Old Gaston, he can cut a couple of holes in it and put it on his donkey.

Suzy (*snatching the hat back*) You'll do no such thing. You may need it one day.

Peter What for, a funeral?

Suzy For some formal occasion, a christening perhaps... Or a wedding. (*She puts the hat back on to the hatstand*)

Peter finishes his drink

Peter Like another?

Suzy No, thanks.

Peter Well, I do. (*He moves to recharge his glass*)
Suzy Before you know it, you'll be drunk.
Peter Euphoria makes a man thirsty. How was Digne?
Suzy Busy. And buzzing with excitement. I think Antoine might have been
   wrong.
Peter What about?
Suzy About German agents preparing the way. About sabotage.

Peter turns to stare at her

   There's been some sort of explosion in a factory north of here. A munitions
   factory. A lot are saying it was deliberate.
Peter You would expect an accident in a munitions factory.
Suzy I'm just repeating what people are saying. So Antoine could be wrong,
   and you could be right. About a war coming. You know, for the first time
   since we met, I wish I were back in England.
Peter If a war does come, nowhere will be safe.
Suzy Yes, but to be back again among one's own people? Don't you ever
   yearn for that, Peter?
Peter I can't go back.
Suzy Can't?
Peter My job is here.
Suzy What job? You can paint anywhere.

Peter moves to touch her

Peter You are down in the dumps, aren't you? I reckon it's the weather, these
   damp, dark days, but Spring is just around the corner, *and* we have a bottle
   of wine to finish. (*He moves to take her glass*)
Suzy No...
Peter I insist. I had a triumph today, Suzy, a weight was lifted, I won't let
   you bring me down. Here. (*He proffers the glass*) Take it.

She does

   Drink.

She does—a sip

   That's better, and next I'm going to make a superb ham salad, *which you
   will eat*. And then to bed, eh ... and then...? In brand new bedsheets, eh?
   You leave 'em in the car? It won't take me a few minutes to sprint down
   and get them...

Suzy I didn't get any bedsheets.
Peter No?
Suzy I lied to you, Peter.
Peter Lied?
Suzy Yes, I went to Digne, but not to buy bedsheets. I went to see a doctor.
Peter What? Why? Dear God, you're not ill, are you?
Suzy No, it's not an illness, it's perfectly natural. I'm pregnant.

Peter stares at her

    Two months. The baby is due in November.
Peter Ohmygod, ohmygod… Ohmygod…
Suzy If you say that again I think I will kill you.
Peter It's … It's a shock … Are you sure?
Suzy Yes, Peter, I am sure, so is the doctor.
Peter My God, this ./. this is ./. unexpected /.. it changes things.
Suzy I hope it will change many things.
Peter I'll stand by you, of course, naturally.
Suzy That's comforting to hear. "Stand by me."
Peter I have to think.
Suzy What is there to think about? I am to become a mother, and you a father.
    I'm ready for it, are you?
Peter I have to think about us.
Suzy I hoped you would.
Peter November? How much grace does that leave us?
Suzy Grace?
Peter It's so damned … inconvenient.
Suzy Inconvenient?
Peter I don't mean that as it sounds. I'm not making sense.
Suzy Oh, but you are, perfect sense.
Peter Suzy…
Suzy (*overriding*) All the way back I thought, I wondered, as to how you
    would take the news, what you would say. I thought you might say
    splendid, terrific, or even marvellous. But not "inconvenient"…
Peter Darling…
Suzy Is there anything else you want to raise or discuss?
Peter Discuss?
Suzy In light of the news that I am going to have your baby, *our* baby?
Peter I'm pleased, darling, of course I am…
Suzy But not pleased enough, Peter. Not sincerely. I'm sorry to be an
    "inconvenience". I am going to bed now, between old bedsheets. (*She*
    moves to the internal door)
Peter Suzy.

Suzy Stay up, Peter, have your feast, finish your wine, and perhaps when you
have a moment, you can ponder on a name for the baby. It should begin
with a B.
Peter B?
Suzy For "bastard".

Suzy exits through the internal door

*Peter is still in a state of shock and confusion. He drains his drink, pours
another, then absently, his mind elsewhere, he takes up a knife, cuts some
bread, opens the ham, and, with his back to us, carves a slice that, when he
turns to us, he pops on to the bread, the knife still in his hand. He moves to
sit down at the table, eating, and yet somehow, by rote, mechanically*

The stable door rattles. Peter alerts, stands up, knife in hand

The top half of the stable door opens and Josef stands there excitedly

Josef It all came back to me. I remember now!

*Peter moves to open the door. Josef enters and homes right in on the bread
and ham and starts to munch away at them. Peter coldly regards him for a
moment*

Peter Josef?

Josef turns

You remembered?
Josef Oh, yes, I thought and I thought and suddenly I remembered. Aren't
I clever?
Peter What did you remember?
Josef I saw you.
Peter What do you think you saw?
Josef You and him. I saw you. Saw you! (*He starts to skip around the area
like a malevolent gnome*) I know what you did, I know what you did, I know
what you did!
Peter Josef.

Josef stops dancing

Did you tell anyone else about this?
Josef No, it's our secret. Divide and conquer. Divide and conquer.

Peter That's good, Josef, that's very good. But we don't want to disturb Suzy, do we?

Josef Suzy`s nice to me, I brought her flowers. I think?

Peter We are a team, aren't we, you and I?

Josef A team, yes.

Peter Nobody else knows our secrets.

Josef Nobody. (*Beat*) I know your secret, I know what you did.

Peter Yes, indeed you do. I think we should talk about this, Josef. But not here. Somewhere quiet.

Josef Quiet, yes. Shh!

Peter opens the stable door, puts his arm around Josef's shoulder and starts to urge him away

Peter Somewhere no-one else can see or hear us.

They exit through the stable door together. The door closes

CURTAIN

ACT II

Scene 1

The Curtain rises on the cottage. Morning. Some months later

It is empty. Nearby are a few new paintings of houses. There is a new rug on the floor

Peter enters through the internal door, wearing work clothes and carrying a battered valise which he puts down on the table, and checks through it, reacts, and exits through the internal door again

Suzy enters through the stable door. She is now heavily pregnant and showing it, her belly swollen. She carries a basket, puts it down, wearily grips her lower back with both hands, then proceeds to take some eggs out of the basket and put them away

Peter enters through the internal door, carrying folded dungarees

Peter You were up early, I told you to lie in. You shouldn't be doing that.
Suzy No? I'll just ring for the butler, shall I? Someone has to feed the chickens and collect the eggs.
Peter I could have done it. How many anyway?
Suzy No threat to the local economy, just five.

Peter sets about making a simple lunch of bread and cheese

Peter Probably that damned fox putting them off.
Suzy What are you doing?
Peter I'll need lunch on the road.
Suzy I'll do it.
Peter You should rest.
Suzy I'm not an invalid. *(She takes over preparing and wrapping the lunch)* Are you picking up Gaston?
Peter Yes, he'll give me a shout from the end of the path. *(He looks at his watch)* Should be here soon.
Suzy I don't think it was a fox, looked more like rats.

Peter Eh?

Suzy The earth down by the cesspit has been disturbed.

Peter Buggers are probably digging in.

Suzy It looked more as though something was tunnelling out.

Peter (*reacting*) I'd better take a look.

Suzy It'll keep, surely?

Peter I'll be gone a few days; don't want you to have any trouble while I'm away.

Peter exits through the stable door

Pause

Suzy finishes the lunch pack, wraps it and moves to pop it into the valise—looks at the new paintings, picks one up, and sits down to study it

Peter re-enters

Peter enters through the stable door

Might be you're right, it could be rats.

Suzy I thought you'd dealt with them.

Peter (*hesitating*) Yes, so did I. But that was months ago, nothing lasts forever.

Suzy No. (*Beat*) On the other hand, it might have been Josef, up to his old tricks.

Peter Why on earth would Josef be digging into the cesspit?

Suzy I don't know, but don't you find it curious that we haven't seen hide nor hair of him in ages?

Peter I've seen him. He just hasn't been around here, that's all. Bothering you. I said I would talk to him, and I did. (*Noting the painting she still holds*) *Pause* It's yours for twenty-five francs. Or, in your case, Madam, a big smile and a kiss! (*He inclines for a kiss but she does not respond*)

Suzy I'm not sure about this.

Peter Oh my God, spare me—a critic!

Suzy I don't know why you gave up painting what you did best.

Peter I got bored, needed a new challenge. One has to move on, darling.

Suzy Yes. One has to move on.

Peter Look, are you sure you're going to be OK while I'm gone?

Suzy I'll be fine. I *feel* fine. A bit tired perhaps, but that's to be expected. Anyway, the baby isn't due for two months.

Peter I wish we had neighbours who were nearer. Or a phone.

Suzy You don't have to worry, I can stand on my own two feet.

Peter That sounds unfashionably independent.

Suzy Because I've been thinking hard, about being independent. I think times are about to change, Peter, that old saw about every woman needs a man to lean on…

Peter Hey! That's pretty radical!

Suzy Just facing up to circumstances. I took the car into town yesterday.
Peter I know you did, to stock up.
Suzy While I was there I contacted my Aunt Jemima.
Peter Jemima? You've never mentioned her before. Who is she, some dried-up old spinster who crouches over her embroidery?
Suzy She is a spinster, yes. She lives in Cornwall, miles from anywhere—a pariah, ostracised by the rest of the family, but she's comfortable, enjoys a good living from her smallholding and is happy in the company of her fifteen-year-old son, who was born out of wedlock! She doesn't make judgments on people, and is more than willing to take me in.
Peter What are you talking about?
Suzy Us, no, me, *my* future. I've made my decision; I'll have our baby, Peter, then I'm leaving you. I am returning to England with the child.
Peter You can't just... We have to talk this over!
Suzy What is there to talk about?
Peter What if I marry you?
Suzy Coerced, forced into it? That wouldn't work, and you know it.
Peter Suzy...
Male Voice (*far off*) M'sieur Meredith? Peter!?
Peter Dammit, that's Gaston. I'm not leaving it here, we have to discuss this.
Suzy I've made up my mind.
Peter I won't accept that.
Male Voice (*far off*) Peter?
Peter I won't let you do this.
Male Voice (*far off*) Peter!
Peter There's still a lot to say...
Male Voice (*far off*) Peter!

Peter opens the door and shouts off

Peter All right, I'm coming! Suzy, I have to go.
Suzy One of us does.

Peter moves to embrace her, but she turns her face away

Peter Soon as I get back we'll thrash this out... Suzy... Oh, damn!

Peter grabs his valise and exits through the stable door

Suzy gazes after him. We hear the tinny sound of car engine start up, move away. Suzy grabs her belly, caresses it

Suzy Oh, my baby— (*She reacts*) Don't kick me! I think we both need some rest, then later I'll take you down to where the poppies grow...

Suzy exits through the internal door

A long pause, then there is a tap at the door, pause, another tap

Finally the door is tried, opens and Ross enters! He is exactly as we recall him, save that now, instead of a suit, he wears the "County" clothes of an English gentleman: twill trousers, tweed hacking jacket, checked shirt, and cravat

Ross Hallo. Hallo? Is there anybody here? (*He moves deeper into the area*) Hallo?

Silence, he looks around, sees one of the paintings, picks it up to examine it

Suzy (*off*) Who is it?

Suzy enters through the internal door

A reaction, each startled by the other

Ross Ma'am, I do beg your pardon. Unforgivable I know, but I knocked and called, and the door was open...
Suzy Who are you, what do you want?
Ross My name is Ross, Arnold Ross. Forgive me, ma'am, but have we met before? Do I seem at all familiar to you?
Suzy No, should you?
Ross I was just hoping. Whom do I have the pleasure of addressing?
Suzy Suzy Hinchcliffe.
Ross Well, Mrs Hinchcliffe...
Suzy *Miss.*

Ross reacts, noting her swollen belly

Ross I see. Miss Hinchcliffe, you asked what I want—at this moment I would be most obliged for a glass of water.
Suzy You're a complete stranger, come barging into my home...
Ross The door was open. I assure you I mean you no harm, I am just a weary, thirsty traveller, but I can see your point, I had no right ... excuse me. (*He moves as though to exit*)
Suzy Oh, for heaven's sake, the water is there. Help yourself.
Ross Thank you. Most kind. (*He moves to get himself some water and drinks*)
I am staying at the hotel up on the hill there, you must know it?
Suzy I know it, I used to work there.

Ross Ah.

Suzy What *are* you doing here?

Ross Do you have a moment, Miss Hinchcliffe?

Suzy I'm running out of patience.

Ross I understand, quite so. Let me explain. I have been staying at the hotel for several days now, and each day I have set off to walk north, south, east … today my direction was west … which brought me to your cottage.

Suzy Are you making a map, conducting some kind of survey?

Ross In a manner of speaking, I am making a survey. Of the immediate area.

Suzy Would you please get to the point?!

Ross My brother.

Suzy Your brother?

Ross He has disappeared, gone missing. After a great deal of effort, I traced him to the station here, then to that charming little bistro on the square.

Suzy The Montmartre.

Ross The Montmartre, yes. After that the trail goes cold, no sign of him since. You appreciate that I am very concerned. Hence I have been back-tracking in all directions, but so far, have accomplished nothing. I've knocked at doors, questioned along the way, but he seems to have vanished altogether. Into thin air.

Suzy How long has he been missing?

Ross Almost exactly five months. He was last seen on Tuesday the eighth of April. I know it is a long while ago, and it is unlikely, but you might have seen *something*—I suppose you wouldn't happen to recall just what *you* were doing that day?

Suzy I recall exactly. At around ten thirty that morning, I drove to Digne.

Ross That's remarkable, in a place as timeless as this, that you can exactly remember one particular day…

Suzy I was going to see my doctor. He confirmed my pregnancy, a woman doesn't forget a thing like that.

Ross Serendipity. But wait a moment, if you drove to Digne you would take the top road towards the town, wouldn't you? You might have seen him en route?

Suzy I might, but how on earth would I have known it was him?

Ross Miss Hinchcliffe, I asked if I seemed familiar to you, because my brother and I are twins, identical, see me you've seen him. Well?

Suzy No. I don't think I passed anyone along the way…

Ross He would have been conspicuous, he was wearing city clothes.

Suzy City clothes?

Ross Yes, you know, dark suit, tie, hat.

Suzy (*her mind racing*) No, I saw no-one like that. But…

Ross But?

Suzy Peter might have seen him.

Ross Peter?

Suzy Peter Meredith, my husb—the man I share this cottage with.

Ross Where is he? How can I reach him?

Suzy He's away for the next few days, I'm not sure for how long.

Ross How can I get in touch with him, then?

Suzy You can't, he's working. Casual labour. Fruit picking, he moves from farm to farm, wherever the work is.

Ross I had intended to return home tomorrow, but perhaps I should now wait. You understand, don't you, any lead to help me find my brother must be pursued?

Suzy Why would your brother disappear? Was he ill, or in trouble?

Ross My brother was in the rudest of good health, and without a care in the world.

Suzy Look, why don't you leave me your address, a number to call, and when Peter returns, I'll ask him to get in touch with you.

Ross That is very kind. And I might take you up on it. Meanwhile, I'll carry on searching.

Suzy Where? There's no-one beyond us for miles.

Ross On my way here I passed a house, well, more of a lean-to actually, a hovel.

Suzy That's Josef's place.

Ross Josef?

Suzy A neighbour.

Ross Well, I'll try and catch up with him on my way back. I'm pleased to know the place *is* occupied; it looked rather derelict to me.

Suzy That's Josef, even when he's home it looks derelict. He often takes off for days on end—and even if you catch up with him, I doubt it'll do you any good.

Ross Oh?

Suzy Josef is … well … a little addled. Nice enough, but addled. He won't recall what he did this morning, let alone five months ago.

Ross You never know. I'm snatching at straws at the moment—anything that might help me locate my brother. I am most obliged to you for your assistance, Miss Hinchcliffe. If anything else occurs to you, well, you know where to find me. Thank you for your time… (*He moves to the stable door*)

Suzy Mr Ross.

He pauses

What is your brother's Christian name?

Ross I am Arnold, he is Frederick.

Suzy F.R.

Ross Eh?

Suzy homes in on the hatstand, to rummage amongst it, and comes out holding the trilby hat

Suzy F.R., The initials here inside the brim. (*She hands it to him*) That's your brother's hat, isn't it?

Ross Yes, where did you find——

Suzy (*overriding*) Peter found it on the back road, found it that day, April the eighth.

Ross (*examining the hat*) The back road? That's the one that skirts the poppy field, isn't it? The one I just walked?

Suzy Yes.

Ross It passes by your neighbour's place, on to here, then where does it go?

Suzy Nowhere. It's an old goat track, leads to the stream then stops. So, he might have been coming *here*. But why?

Ross This could be vital, a straw to be snatched at! If this "Peter" can show me exactly where he found it… You see now, how important it is that I talk to him?

Suzy I'll put him in touch as soon as he returns.

Ross But you don't know when that will be?

Suzy Tomorrow, day after tomorrow, a week from now … it all depends on the weather and the crop.

Ross This at least confirms that Frederick *was* here. I have a colleague back at the hotel, who is assisting me, we must discuss this. (*He opens the stable door*)

Suzy Mr Ross?

He pauses

"A colleague"? Two bloodhounds on the same trail? Why? What do you really think may have happened to your brother?

Ross I hope and pray nothing, but one cannot rule out foul play.

Suzy Foul play?!

Ross My brother was alone, vulnerable, and carrying a large amount of money.

Ross exits through the stable door

Suzy stares after him, hugging herself, troubled, perplexed

Black-out

Scene 2

The Lights come up on the cottage. Early evening, later that day

The room is empty for a moment. The main Lights are on

Suzy enters through the stable door, carrying some fresh picked produce: herbs or asparagus. She takes them to the sink area and begins to clean them

We hear a car approaching, to come up and stop. Suzy reacts in surprise

Suzy Peter? (*She hurries to open the door*)

She is confronted by Ross and Miriam Miller. Miriam is in her forties, a forthright woman

Ross Miss Hinchcliffe, may we come in?

Suzy pulls the door wider, Ross and Miriam enter

Sorry to disturb you again, but we do think it important. This is my colleague, Miriam Miller.

Miriam Miss Hinchcliffe, so pleased to meet you. My dear, you seem somewhat surprised.

Suzy I... I somehow didn't expect you to be——

Miriam (*intejecting*) A woman? Times are changing, you know. A woman's touch, a woman's intuition? We are starting to be appreciated at last.

Ross I do apologize for the intrusion, we hope not to take up too much of your time.

Suzy It's all right. Frankly, I would welcome the company.

Miriam Yes, this is quite a lonely place, isn't it?

Suzy Can I offer you some wine, or coffee?

Ross Well, perhaps a glass of wine would be——

Miriam (*overriding*) No. Neither, thank you. We should not impose, Arnold, also, a clear head, eh? This is serious business. We'll try not to keep you too long, my dear, you look tired. How long do you have to go?

Suzy About two months.

Miriam The last weeks are the worst, when you feel you have had enough of carrying that thing around, that it will never end. I know, I had one of my own, a fine strapping man now, and a credit to his country.

Suzy How can I help you?

Ross Miss Hinchcliffe, that day—the eighth of April—can you recall anything else different about that day?

Suzy Well... Peter drank the Latour.

Ross A Château Latour?

Suzy Yes, it was one of a pair we'd been saving. He'd made a big sale that day, you see, to an American. He was very ... euphoric.

Ross This American, did he come here?

Suzy I don't think so. Perhaps. Why?

Ross Another person who might have seen my brother.

Miriam A big sale you said, so he made quite a lot of money?

Suzy Yes, he got rid of all his poppy paintings.

Ross and Miriam exchange a look

Ross He paints poppies?

Suzy Not any more. (*She indicates the new pictures*) As you can see, he changed his subject.

Miriam He sold all of them to this American?

Suzy All except one.

Miriam Where is that?

Suzy I have it in the bedroom.

Ross Could we see it?

Suzy I don't see how that can have any bearing on——

Ross (*interjecting*) Miss Hinchcliffe, it may be pertinent. Humour me. Please.

Suzy (*shrugging*) Very well.

Suzy exits through the internal door Pause

Ross What do you think?

Miriam I think she is an intelligent young woman, and we will have to tell her the truth.

Ross As we discussed?

Miriam As we discussed.

Ross The Latour could be significant. You know Frederick's taste.

Suzy enters through the internal door, carrying a poppy painting

Miriam takes it, studies it, hands it to Ross // Pause

Miriam You were more familiar with them than I.

Ross Looks very similar.

Suzy Similar! Would you please explain to me what is going on?

Ross Miss Hinchclifie, how did this American pay? Was it in traveller's cheques? Dollars?

Suzy No, it was in francs.

Miriam Francs. And quite a large sum you say?

Suzy I'm not sure quite how much, it was a wad of notes.

Ross (*to Miriam*) A wad.

Suzy Look, I want to help, but I am tired of you talking in riddles!

Miriam I'm sorry, my dear, but we haven't been entirely truthful with you—about who we really are. I am Superintendent Miller, and this is Chief Inspector Ross.

Suzy Police?!

Miriam We have, of course, no jurisdiction here, but are investigating the disappearance of Arnold's brother, who also holds the rank of Chief Inspector.

Suzy But how could this possibly involve me or Peter?

Miriam I am sure *you* are innocent. But Peter... Meredith, is it not?

Suzy Yes.

Miriam We think that he has been deceiving you, and that is not his name at all.

Ross We think he is in fact Giles Hudson.

Suzy Hudson? Who is he?

Ross Doesn't the name mean anything to you? It was in all the papers.

Miriam Come now, Arnold, she is very young, and it happened quite a while ago—and far from here.

Suzy For pity's sake! What happened? Who is Hudson?

Miriam A particularly vicious criminal. He murdered his wife and child in the most appalling circumstances!

Suzy You can't imagine that Peter and this — this killer are one and the same?!

Ross We are rapidly coming to that conclusion—the facts fit.

Suzy That's ridiculous.

Miriam When did you first meet him?

Suzy Four years ago. I was on a student holiday...

Miriam (*to Ross*) Four years.

Ross Hudson escaped from prison just over four years ago.

Suzy That could be just a coincidence, and these "facts" you spoke of, what are they?

Ross My brother was carrying money, Peter came into money. Frederick lost his hat. Peter found it here. Frederick loved Latour, Peter drank Latour. That day. And this picture... (*He proffers the poppy painting*) Peter's work—and something very like them were found on the walls of the cell Hudson escaped from.

Suzy sways a little, Miriam grips her

Miriam Sit down, my dear. I know this has been a great shock. Arnold, see if you can find some brandy—pregnant or not, she needs some.

Suzy No, I'll be fine.
Miriam Let's try to be quite sure. Arnold.

Ross produces a photo, shows it to Suzy

This is a photo of Giles Hudson.

Suzy stares at it

Ross Well?
Suzy He's bearded. And the hair colour is wrong.
Ross Those can be altered.
Suzy The face. It's Peter's *kind* of face, but it isn't—it's different.
Ross We think it likely that Hudson underwent some kind of facial surgery.
Miriam *Could* that be Peter?
Suzy I don't know. Possibly.
Ross Let's compare with Peter as he is now, you must have some photos?
Suzy Yes… No. I… I took some when we first met but — but Peter lost them.
    (*She stares at them—she is beginning to accept the unacceptable*) How did
    Hudson escape?
Ross We are still not sure, we think he had inside help, there were several
    of them went over the wall that night
Suzy Was the wall protected?
Ross Eh?
Suzy Was there barbed wire?
Ross Yes, and judging from the blood, one or other of them got caught up
    on it. Why do you ask?
Suzy Peter has scars on his back. (*She buries her face in her hands*)
Miriam Arnold, the brandy.

*Ross moves to find and pour a brandy, hands it to Suzy. She drinks and
regains control*

Suzy (*more forthrightly*) No, it can't be Peter, he's good and kind…
Miriam Miss Hinchcliffe, you are with child—but unmarried. Why?

Suzy reacts, paces away, clutching her belly

Suzy How did Hudson kill his wife?
Miriam With a knife.
Suzy Murderers don't change their methods, do they?
Ross Who knows? In a moment of desperation, he might use the first means
    at hand. Why?

Suzy That day Peter had been using rat poison.

Miriam and Ross look at each other

Miriam ⎫ (*together*) In the Latour!
Ross ⎭
Miriam What else do you recall?
Suzy The rug was gone. Not that one, the old one.
Ross About this size, was it?
Suzy Yes.
Ross (*to Miriam*) Ideal to wrap a body in.
Miriam Yes, but where would he take it?
Ross You have a car?
Suzy Yes, but I was using it that day. (*She realizes*) Oh, my God—he was
wearing work clothes, he was muddy, he said he'd been working on the
cesspit. Is that where he is? Could your brother be buried out there?!
Ross Very possibly, certainly I am now convinced that Frederick is dead, and
that heartless swine did for him!
Suzy I'm so, so sorry.
Miriam So am I. Poor Arnold, you must be mortified—but now it is
imperative that we remember why we are here, and that we re-capture
Hudson and take him back to where he belongs.
Ross You are right, of course, can't let personal emotions intrude. (*To Suzy*)
You are not sure when he's due to return?
Suzy Some night over the next few days.
Miriam At night? It's always at night?
Suzy It always has been. They work while there's daylight, until the last
moment.
Miriam It's as we thought, Arnold. (*To Suzy*) We discussed this eventuality
already.
Ross Hudson must be taken, with no possibility of him getting away again.
Miriam We can't stake out this place twenty-four hours a day, for goodness
knows how long. For one thing, he might detect something, be alerted.
Ross We can't take that chance. When we make our move it has to be sure,
swift, and final!
Miriam You will have to help us, my dear. Are you up to it?
Suzy Help betray Peter?
Miriam I'd hoped to spare you the details of his crime! But now I fear I must
tell you—so you will understand what kind of beast you may have qualms
about betraying. Giles Hudson took a kitchen knife and didn't just stab his
wife. She was, like you, heavily pregnant. He stabbed her many times—
in the belly—killing their unborn child too.
Suzy Why would a man do that?

Miriam Our medical team had a theory—jealousy.

Suzy Jealous of what?

Miriam The child she was carrying; somehow in his diseased mind it had become a threat, a competitor for her undivided love.

Suzy But that's insane.

Ross We think he is.

Miriam Well?

Suzy What would I have to do?

Miriam We can see this place from our hotel. The door, and the window. This window. (*She moves to the window above the sink*) When he returns, the electric light will not be functioning.

Suzy But how?

Miriam (*overriding*) Arnold will disable the generator, so the only light will be that of these oil lamps. You must behave normally—how do you usually welcome him?

Suzy With a drink. Coffee, or wine.

Miriam Could not be better. Right, you will bring him that drink, but before you do, you will slip one of these pills into it. (*She produces some pills*)

Suzy stares at them

Suzy They won't——

Miriam (*overriding*) Kill him? No, my dear, that would defeat our purpose. But it will disable him, render him incapable. And then... Arnold?

Arnold picks up and brings a large oil lamp and places it on the sill above the sink and under the window

Make sure the curtains are drawn back, and place the lamp here. One of us will be on watch up there throughout the hours of darkness. As soon as we see your signal, we will drive down and deal with him. We will take him away, and you will never have to see him again.

Suzy stares at them

Do you think you can do it?

Suzy I can try.

Ross You have to be damned sure!

Miriam Arnold! (*To Suzy*) So long as you keep calm and make sure he suspects nothing, you won't be in any danger—and after you have given him the pill it won't matter, he will be helpless.

Ross produces and flourishes handcuffs

Ross I'll say!

Miriam You will do this for us, won't you, dear?

Suzy (*hesitating*) Peter's the father of my child. Are you *sure* he's the man?

Miriam After all we have discovered here tonight, yes, we are sure. And, although you can't bring yourself to admit it, I think you are too.

Suzy Yes.

Miriam I know what we are asking is hard for you/

Suzy I'll do it. I'll do exactly as you say.

Ross Remember, as soon as we see a lamp in that window we'll be on our way.

Miriam She understands, Arnold. She is a very brave young woman. (*She moves to grip Suzy*) Just hold on a little longer, my dear, until he returns, then it will be over.

Ross And we'll have our man at last.

Suzy Don't you mean, *my* man?

Black-out

SCENE 3

The Lights come up on the cottage. That night

The stage is lit by the oil lamp only. Author's note: please take dramatic licence, and not make the set so dim that essential action is not clearly seen

Suzy enters through the internal door, and moves to tidy a few plates and glasses up and stack them for washing later

She surveys the area, then moves and is about to turn out the oil lamp when she hears the tinny engine of a car approaching, stopping. She turns towards the door

Suzy Peter?

A moment, then the stable door opens and Peter enters

Peter!

He moves to switch on the radio, but it isn't working, He tries a light switch

Peter What the hell? Why aren't the lights working?

Suzy The generator's defunct.

Peter I'd better take a look… (*He moves to exit*)

Suzy It's no use—it's … run out of fuel.

Peter Didn't you check?

Suzy I meant to. I forgot.

Peter Damn!

Suzy What's so vital?

Peter I wanted to get the World Service, that's all. Something's up, something important. I've been hearing rumours all the way home.

Suzy Why are you home so soon? You've been gone less than twenty-four hours.

Peter I know.

Suzy What was it, did the crops fail?

Peter On the contrary, everything is ripe and blooming—abundant.

Suzy Then why?

Peter I cut it short, damn the money, there are things more important! We have some unfinished business, you and I, Suzy. Christ, I'm hungry!

Suzy I'll get you something.

Peter No, you sit down, I'll fix it. (*As he speaks, he picks up a long knife and starts to find and cut bread*)

Suzy A drink, then?

Peter Later. I was up a tree, picking fruit, and suddenly thought, it might as well be a gum tree.

Suzy is baffled

I'm up a gum tree, got it? It's the baby.

Suzy The baby?

Peter That little bastard you're carrying in your belly, that's what's brought all this to a head.

Suzy What do you mean?

Peter I mean *us*—and it—that's what's upset the apple cart—disturbed the status quo. God, Suzy, these past few years we've been happy, poor, yes, but happy—and now *that* has come along, I'm not going to be Number One around here any more, am I? Going to be replaced by the pitter patter of a little stranger, and new responsibilities. I have to do something about that … and I've decided just what. (*He turns and moves towards her with the knife*)

Suzy is terrified

Yes, I've made up my mind what I have to do. Something I should have done when you first told me you were pregnant. Face up to the situation and deal with it. (*As he talks, he emphasizes his words with knife in hand—in what could be construed as a threatening manner*)

Suzy backs away in fear

I've been fooling myself, avoiding the issue, but it isn't going to go away, so I'll have to attack it head on. (*He moves much closer*)

Suzy squeals and pulls away. Peter stares at her

Suzy? (*He steps closer*)

Suzy steps back

What the devil is the matter with you?

Suzy You're frightening me.

Peter With my passion? You never minded before? But you're right. I promised myself I'd deal with it in a calm and collected fashion—cold and clear about what I must do. I'll need all your understanding, because, whatever happens, I do love you, Suzy. Always will. Remember that?

Suzy I'd like a drink. Wouldn't you?

Peter Yes, perhaps I do need a drink first—Dutch courage. But not the Latour! This is too sombre an occasion.

Suzy moves to pick up the lamp and put it on the sill above the sink. Then she pours two glasses of wine

There are things you don't know about me, Suzy, dark things. Things you would never have suspected. Nothing will ever be the same again, I'm resigned to that. Nothing.

Suzy is about to put the pill in his glass, he glances back at her, she "covers" her actions

I'm sorry but it has to be. (*He turns back again*)

Suzy drops the pill into his glass

All the way home I've been thinking about it.

Suzy hands him his glass of wine. He stares into it, not drinking yet

This may be the hardest thing I've ever had to do.

Suzy clinks her glass against his

Suzy Santé!

She drinks. Peter does not

Peter?

Peter I'm not Peter. My real name is Giles Hudson! And I once had a wife.

Suzy stares at him

You took that rather well! Everything you thought you knew about me has been a lie. (*He takes a sip of his drink*) Except for the painting; I've always done that, but by profession I was an architect. Back in 1934 I was commissioned to help revamp the British Embassy in Berlin, lived there for quite a while. My wife came over to join me. She was a fine woman and, like you, she was pregnant, close to her time. (*He takes another sip of wine*) One day a man came to me, a doctor. For whatever reason, our diplomats were ignoring him but he thought that I, with my Embassy connections, might be able to help. He told me his wife was Jewish, and she had been arrested, along with his two children, and taken to some secret camp. I wasn't inclined to take him seriously. But then he took me for a drive, a long, long drive, at the end of which we got to the camp. It wasn't easy, the place was teeming with guards, but I saw it for myself, if I hadn't I would never have believed it—what one human being could do to another. (*He takes a long drink now*) He said the world should know what was going on, and I agreed with him. But no-one would believe me, and I could understand why, you couldn't imagine that camp, you had to see it! I just knew it had to be stopped. So we came up with a plan, the man and I, and a few others. An architect is exposed to many skills, including demolition. I made a bomb. It would have worked too, but we were betrayed, and all of us arrested, and came under the tender care of their Gestapo. (*He downs the rest of the wine, moves to pour another*)

Suzy can only stand, stare, listen, like a snake with a mongoose

Their tortures ranged from the refined to the brutal.

Suzy Tortures?

Peter You've seen the scars on my back. The doctor they sent mad. But it was me they really wanted.

Suzy Because you were the ring-leader?

Peter Because I was *British*. They wanted a confession, a show trial, *a reason*.

Suzy Reason for what?

Peter For Hitler to hold the British Government accountable—perhaps even a reason to declare war against us.

Suzy Who was that bomb intended for?

Peter We theorised that, cut off the head, the body would then die.

Suzy You mean?

Peter Adolf Hitler, we were going to assassinate Hitler! And we came this close. They beat me. But I beat them, broke out one night and went to ground. At least I thought I'd beaten them. They murdered my wife, and the child she was carrying, and framed me for it. Intent, you see, on making me an outcast, unable to go home, to get help from anyone, while all the while they were searching for me. That's why I resisted marrying you. My papers are false, they'll pass casual scrutiny—but when you get married, they need more details, birth certificates … and so on. The Gestapo never give up, Suzy. Some months ago, the day you went to Digne, one of them found me, and I killed him, poisoned him, then, God forgive me, finished him off with my bare hands! Only the man knew.

Suzy What man?

Peter The doctor. The man they sent mad. Josef!

Suzy Oh, dear God, what have I done?

Peter Suzy…

Suzy Ross was here.

Peter Ross? What the hell do you know about Ross?!

Suzy He came here today, with a woman named Miller.

Peter Miller? Her name is Muller! She's Gestapo, so are the Ross twins, despite their accent, which is courtesy of a British education. So I killed Tweedledee—and Tweedledum showed up… What did he want? (*He staggers, grips the sofa for support*) I feel a bit odd. Groggy. We have to get away from here, Suzy. *Now!*

Suzy It may be too late. (*She draws the curtain, takes the lamp and puts it elsewhere*)

Peter What do you mean?

Suzy They gave me something to put in your drink.

Peter (*getting less* compos mentis *all the time*) What? What!

Suzy It won't kill you, they promised me that, but you will soon be helpless. They could be here any moment.

Peter takes a step towards her, then collapses on to the sofa

Peter You must go.

Suzy No.

Peter Don't you understand, you're a witness? They won't want witnesses. *Go!*

Suzy I'm not leaving you.

Peter Then call Josef, he's out there on watch somewhere. Call him! (*He sinks back, he is very close to unconsciousness, and not quite* compos mentis)

Suzy moves to open the stable door

Suzy Josef! Josef! (*She slams the door shut and returns to Peter*)
Peter Suzy … up there … behind the Latour…

Suzy, baffled, moves to take out the bottle of Latour, and rummages behind it, eventually she comes up with a wrapped bundle that contains Ross's gun

Don't let them take me alive…
Suzy Oh, darling…
Peter Promise me! (*He flops back*)

Suzy puts the gun down, starts to shake him, slaps his cheeks

Suzy You have to stay awake. Peter. Peter!

He opens glazed eyes

You can't go to sleep. Water! (*She hurries to get water*) You have to drink. Oh my darling… (*She puts water to his mouth*)

He takes some, gurgles, spills some. She persists in trying pour it into him

More! Hold on, oh, please, Peter, for God's sake hold on! (*She grabs him, and with difficulty pulls him to his feet*) Walk.

Peter tries a few stumbling steps, then sags, she can't support him, and he falls to the floor

No. (*She crouches beside him, shaking him awake*)

The stable door slams open, Josef enters, to stand there, his gun slung across his back

Josef! Help me.

Josef moves to her

Get him to his feet.

Between them they manage to get Peter on his feet, but he is almost a deadweight

Josef (*giggling*) Peter's drunk. Peter's drunk.
Suzy No, he's not, he's in trouble. And he's your friend, isn't he? Your friend?

Josef Peter's kind. Good to me.

Suzy And he's in danger, do you understand, we have to get him away from here? Can you do that, Josef, can you take him into the woods and hide him?

Josef The woods?

With Peter between them, Josef steers towards the stable door

Suzy No, not that way. Out the back door. (*She steers Peter around towards the internal door*) Take him, hide him, and stay with him until I call. Have you got that?

Josef Divide and conquer.

Suzy spins round as she hears the sound of a car approaching

Suzy You must hurry. Drag him if you have to, but get him away from here!

Josef, half-supporting, half-dragging a stumbling Peter, exits through the internal door

There is the sound of a car coming up. It stops and the car doors slam. Suzy grabs the gun, hesitates, then pushes it behind the sofa cushion

Just in time, as Ross and Miriam enter through the stable door

Miriam We saw your signal.

Suzy It was a mistake!

Ross Mistake?

Suzy I wasn't thinking. I was at the sink, put the lamp down... I'm sorry.

Ross Not as sorry as we are.

Miriam So, a false alarm, then?

Suzy Yes.

Miriam Well, better luck next time. Come, Arnold. (*She moves to the stable door*)

Ross makes no move at all

Arnold?

Ross moves to pick up and display the two empty wine glasses

Ross A pregnant woman might allow herself one glass of wine a day. But two?

Miriam Oh, my dear.

Ross Where is he? (*He moves and slaps Suzy hard across the face*) Tell me! He's here, isn't he?

Suzy He was. He's gone, I couldn't stop him.

Miriam "Couldn't"? You wouldn't lie to us, would you, dear?

Suzy Search the place if you wish.

Miriam (*with a vehemence we have never seen before*) Dammit, he *has* gone! You will regret this.

Ross slaps Suzy again

Ross Where did he go? Where!? (*He picks up the knife and moves menacingly in on Suzy to present the knife against her swollen belly*) I did it once before, I can do it again. Answer me!

At this moment Josef enters through the internal door, still supporting the semi-conscious Peter

Josef I forgot where you told me to take him.

A stunned moment as they all turn to look at him. Then Ross grins, moves in—Josef stares at him

No!

Josef lets go of Peter and turns tail, to exit through the internal door

Peter falls to the floor. Ross steps in, regards Peter, then kicks him

Ross So. At last we have Mr Hudson again. *Miriam, werden Sie herzlich die Tür öffnen.* [*Translation: Miriam, if you will kindly open the door.*]

Miriam *Ja, sofort.* [*Translation: Yes, right away.*] (*She pushes the stable door wide*)

Ross bends to lift/drag Peter towards it. Suzy swoops in to grab the gun from behind the cushion and aims it

Suzy No!

They regard her

Miriam I don't think you intend to use that, my dear.

Suzy I won't let you take him.

Ross bends to continue pulling Peter to the door

I'm warning you. I *will* do it!

Ross grins, continues dragging

Stop! (*She is about to fire*)

BANG! A shot crashes out. Ross straightens up, lets Peter fall to the floor, looks at Suzy in surprise

Ross You bloody English! ⁻ now in German .

Ross falls out of the stable door and beyond—dead

A beat later, Josef enters through the internal door, holding his gun

Josef I finally remembered. I think!

A shocked pause, then suddenly the electric lights come back on. Miriam //
reacts to the lights and moves to look off out of the stable door at Ross //
Pause .
Miriam He couldn't even get that right.

The wireless hums back into life

Male BBC Announcer …earlier today, despite his promises, Hitler's army
  invaded Poland. It now seems only a matter of hours before France and
  Great Britain will be at war with Nazi Germany. There has been international
  condemnation at this act of aggression, and Prime Minister Chamberlain
  has urgently summoned a meeting of——

*Miriam switches off the wireless. Both Josef and Suzy now cover her with
their guns, but she seems unconcerned*

Miriam Well. Our mission is redundant now. It seems we will be at war with
  one another without recourse to accusations or show trials. I shall return to
  my home country, and suggest you do the same, my dear. Take your man
  with you. (*She moves to the stable door*)
Suzy What about him!? (*She indicates Ross outside the door*)
Miriam Arnold? The authorities will learn nothing from me, my dear. As
  I said, we have no jurisdiction here—not yet. Bury him with his brother.
  (*She pauses in the stable doorway*) I trust you have a fine, healthy baby,

but who can guess what awaits the poor mite in this uncertain world? If all the British are like you, we may be in for a hard fight.

Miriam exits

Suzy and Josef remain unmoving as they hear a car start up and move away. Then Suzy moves to crouch beside Peter and cradle him

Suzy Josef, you've work to do. Then we must start loading the car. We're going home.

CURTAIN

FURNITURE AND PROPERTY LIST

Further dressing may be added at the director's discretion

ACT I

SCENE 1

On stage: Practical sink. *Near it*: chunk of bread
Stove
Cupboards. *In them*: cheese, funnel
Bulkhead shelf. *On it*: bottles of wine, 2 of Château Latour.
   On top shelf: flit sprays, bottles, packets, rat poison
Waste bin
Small, rough-hewn table
2 wooden chairs
Table. *On it*: bowl of fruit containing apples
Beaten-up old sofa. *On it*: magazines and papers
Hatstand with coats, hats, scarves
Wellington boots, some with walking sticks or umbrellas,
   beret stuffed in one
Pictures on walls
Canvases
Rough, woven rug
Electric wireless
Electric light
Oil lamp
Grapes
Can
Kettle
Coffee
Carrying bag
Long carving knife
Glasses
Tea cloth
Bottle of brandy
Cups
Spices

Off stage: Worn canvas bag, shotgun or rifle (**Josef**)
               Purse (**Suzy**)

Personal: **Peter**: franc notes, wrist-watch (worn throughout)

Scene 2

On stage: As before

Off stage: Bag (**Peter**)
               Bunch of wild flowers (**Josef**)

Personal: **Peter**: beret
               Ross: dark hat, revolver, wallet containing wad of money

Scene 3

On stage: As before

Off stage: Sack (**Peter**)
               Shovel (**Josef**)
               Medium-sized paper sack (**Peter**)
               Wrapped ham (**Peter**)

Personal: **Suzy**: scarf
               Peter: wad of notes

ACT II

Scene 1

Set: New paintings of houses
               New rug

Off stage: Battered valise (**Peter**)
               Basket containing eggs (**Suzy**)
               Folded dungarees (**Peter**)

Scene 2

On stage: As before

Off stage: Fresh herbs or asparagus (**Suzy**)
               Poppy painting (**Suzy**)

Personal: **Ross:** photo
               Miriam: pills
               Ross: handcuffs

SCENE 3

Set: Plates and glasses

Off stage: Gun (**Josef**)

LIGHTING PLOT

Practical fittings required: oil lamps
1 interior. The same throughout

ACT I, Scene 1

To open:	Early morning in April	
Cue 1	**Josef** switches on the lights *Bring up general lighting*	(Page 2)
Cue 2	**Peter** puts the kettle on *Flicker, dim, then fade out lights*	(Page 2)
Cue 3	**Peter**: "…awful, fickle, generator!" *Bring up lights*	(Page 2)
Cue 4	**Suzy** switches off the lights *Fade out lights*	(Page 9)
Cue 5	**Josef** switches on the lights *Bring up lights*	(Page 10)
Cue 6	**Josef**: "Heil Hitler!" *Black-out*	(Page 10)

ACT I, Scene 2

To open:	Morning lighting	
Cue 7	**Peter** drags **Ross** to door *Black-out*	(Page 18)

ACT I, SCENE 3

To open: Morning lighting

No cues

ACT II, SCENE 1

To open: Morning lighting

Cue 8   **Suzy** hugs herself   (Page 36)
             Black-out

ACT II, SCENE 2

To open: Early evening lighting

Cue 9   **Suzy**: "Don't you mean, my man?"   (Page 43)
             Black-out

ACT II, SCENE 3

To open: Oil lamp only, with covering spot

Cue 10   **Josef**: "I finally remembered."   (Page 51)
             Bring up electric lights

EFFECTS PLOT

ACT I

Cue 1 To open Scene 1 (Page 1)
Silence, then sound of cock crowing far off

Cue 2 **Josef** turns on lights (Page 2)
*Turn on wireless with squawk of sound, warming up,
playing French music, occasionally static intervening*

Cue 3 **Peter** adjust wireless (Page 2)
Wireless plays classical music

Cue 4 The lights fade out (Page 2)
Cut wireless

Cue 5 Lights flicker and come on again (Page 2)
Wireless comes back on, playing music

Cue 6 **Peter** moves to table and sits, eating (Page 2)
Wireless loses station

Cue 7 **Peter** adjusts wireless (Page 3)
Male BBC Announcer *on wireless as script page 3,
then station lost again*

Cue 8 **Peter** re-tunes the wireless (Page 3)
Male German Announcer *on wireless as script page 3*

Cue 9 **Peter** switches it off (Page 3)
Cut wireless

Cue 10 **Suzy** exits (Page 9)
*After a moment the sound of car door slam, tinny engine
of old car starting up and moving away*

Cue 11 **Josef** switches on lights (Page 10)
Wireless warms up, then **Male German Announcer**
as script page 10

Effects Plot

Cue 12   To open Scene 3   (Page 19)
                 Sound of shovel being propped outside stable door

ACT II

Cue 13   **Peter** exits   (Page 32)
                 After a moment, tinny sound of car engine start up,
                    move away

Cue 14   **Suzy** starts preparing food   (Page 37)
                 Sound of car approaching, to come up and stop

Cue 15   **Suzy** is about to blow out one of the oil lamps   (Page 43)
                 Sound of tinny engine of a car approaching, stopping

Cue 16   **Josef**: "Divide and conquer."   (Page 49)
                 Sound of car approaching, to come up and stop

Cue 17   **Suzy**: "Stop!"   (Page 51)
                 Gun shot

Cue 18   **Miriam**: "He couldn't even get that right."   (Page 51)
                 Wireless hums back into life, **Male BBC Announcer**
                    as script page 51

Cue 19   **Miriam** switches off the wireless   (Page 51)
                 Cut wireless

Cue 20   **Miriam** exits   (Page 52)
                 After a moment, sound of car start up and move away